Children are likely to remember the song and "read" it to you because it's familiar and has such a strong pattern. This is all part of learning to read, so don't worry if the words aren't exactly the same as the words on the page.

The pictures tell both the story of Old MacDonald and the story of the piglet's adventure. Children will enjoy the different stories in this book, and it's a way for them to learn that the pictures sometimes "say" more than the words.

And on that farm he had some sheep, E-I-E-I-O!

With a baa there, and a baa here...

Little pig ran all the way home.

"Where have you been?" said his mummy.

a honk honk!

We hope you enjoy reading this book together.

For Peter, Penny and Charlotte

First published 1998 by Walker Books Ltd
87 Vauxhall Walk, London SE11 5HJ

2 4 6 8 10 9 7 5 3 1

Printed in Great Britain

ISBN 0-7445-4896-9

Reading Together

Old MacDonald Had a Farm

Read it together

Old MacDonald Had a Farm is a favourite song for many children. It's a song children love to act out and can be played as a game with friends.

Children enjoy hearing you read familiar songs, rhymes or stories. It helps them to build their confidence with books if they can join in.

Talking together about the song — the words and the pictures — gives children the chance to tell you about the book and ask questions.

Encourage children to join in by leaving them space to finish the rhyme. It's great fun and helps them to listen for the sounds and rhythms in rhymes and songs.

Oh, I know this book. Will you read it?

Yes. You mak the noises.

Splash!

He's chased the ducks into the water.

Here a honk, there a honk, everywhere ...

Old MacDonald Had a Farm

Illustrated by
Jane Chapman

WALKER BOOKS
AND SUBSIDIARIES
LONDON • BOSTON • SYDNEY

Old MacDonald had a farm,
E-I-E-I-O!

And on that farm he had some pigs,
E-I-E-I-O!

With an **oink oink** here and an **oink oink** there

ere an **oink,** there an **oink,** everywhere an **oink** **oink!**

Old MacDonald had a farm,
E-I-E-I-O!

And on that farm he had some ducks,
E-I-E-I-O!

With a **quack quack** here and a **quack quack** there

ere a **quack,** there a **quack,** everywhere a **quack quack!**

Old MacDonald had a farm,
E-I-E-I-O!

And on that farm he had some cows,
E-I-E-I-O!

With a **moo moo** here and a **moo moo** there

ere a **moo,** there a **moo,** everywhere a **moo moo!**

Old MacDonald had a farm,
E-I-E-I-O!

And on that farm he had some hens,
E-I-E-I-O!

With a **cluck cluck** here and a **cluck cluck** there,

here a **cluck,** there a **cluck,** everywhere a **cluck cluck!**

Old MacDonald had a farm,
E-I-E-I-O!

And on that farm he had some sheep,
E-I-E-I-O!

With a **baa baa** here and a **baa baa** there,

here a **baa,** there a **baa,** everywhere a **baa baa!**

Old MacDonald had a farm,
E-I-E-I-O!

And on that farm he had some geese,
E-I-E-I-O!

With a **honk honk** here and a **honk honk** ther

ere a **honk**, there a **honk**, everywhere a **honk honk!**

Old MacDonald had a farm,
E-I-E-I-O!

And on that farm he had a horse,
E-I-E-I-O!

With a neigh neigh here and a neigh neigh there

ere a **neigh**, there a **neigh**, everywhere a **neigh neigh!**

Old MacDonald had a farm,
E-I-E-I-O!

And on that farm he had a . . . dog!

E-I-E-I-O!

With a **woof woof** here and a **woof woof** ther

…ere a **woof**, there a **woof**, everywhere a **woof**
woof!

Old MacDonald had a farm,

E-I-E-I-O!

Read it again

On that farm he had some pigs. One's peeping over the wall, and one gets out.

Retell the story

A good way to remember the story is to retell it using the picture of the farm at the beginning. You could begin by talking through the different parts of the picture together and remembering what happened on Old MacDonald's farm.

Sing it

This traditional song invites children to make animal noises and actions. They can learn it by heart and perform it for you or on to a tape, perhaps with noisy sound effects.

...here a cluck, there a cluck, everywhere a cluck cluck!

Cluck cluck!

And then the ducks flapped their big wings and tried to catch the pig.

The piglet's story

When the piglet runs back home to the pen, there is an exciting tale to tell the others. Children can use toys or puppets to help them retell the story.

Animal noises

Together you could make a set of cards, some with pictures of the animals and others with the sounds they make. With these you can play matching games or sort the cards into the same order as the animals appear in the story.

Make up a song

Children might like to make up their own version of Old MacDonald, perhaps singing about different kinds of animals. For example, "And on that farm he had a goat, E-I-E-I-O". They could also make up their own song using Old MacDonald as a model.

> Father Christmas had a band, E-I-E-I-O!

> And in that band he had a flute, E-I-E-I-O!

Other versions

There are many book versions of this song. They may have different illustrations, animals and endings from this one. In getting to know a variety, you can talk about them together, noticing similarities and differences.

Reading Together

The *Reading Together* series is divided into four levels – starting with red, then on to yellow, blue and finally green. The six books in each level offer children varied experiences of reading. There are stories, poems, rhymes and songs, traditional tales and information books to choose from.

Accompanying the series is a Parents' Handbook, which looks at all the different ways children learn to read and explains how *your* help can really make a difference!

     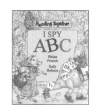